Synthetic Moon

Poetry and Prose

My words are better on paper

By
J.M. Preston

Legal

Synthetic Moon
© John Preston 2020

First Published June 2020

Views expressed In the Poetry Is that of the
Authors Own and does not represent
That of a self-help book. Intended for
Inspirational purposes only

Enquires should be sent to contact@johnprestonpoetry.com
Please visit www.johnprestonpoetry.com for more information
On products.

Please Visit and follow John preston poetry On
Facebook and Instagram for daily verses

Introduction

First and foremost, I like to thank each and every one of you who
support my work and for

Purchasing this book. It truly means the world and beyond to me,
more than what any words

Could ever describe and I sincerely hope that this book can live up
to the standards you have

come to know and love on social media. I truly hope you enjoy
this book; I did however remove a

few old works from this book to make way for some more of my
modern material today.

I wanted to combine the old with the new to more of a positive feel
to this title.

I started writing this book about 3 years back, one night I was

standing outside, I was lost in my problems and I just wanted to
feel something natural and real.

Upon looking up gazing into the beautiful night sky I saw a big
beautiful full moon surrounded by millions

Of tiny bright stars then it hit me that the moon is not synthetic but
instead its real and natural.

Days later, I was walking around at work and it came to me, so I
sat down and wrote

the poem Synthetic Moon.

Table of Contents

Just Not a Song

Love does not work with only one
It is not a game and it's not just a
Song to be sung.

Life is terrible at times, not just hard.
You can give everything and still be
Empty. Life is not a game and it is not
Just a song to be sung.

Too many people are more worried about
Themselves, how hard is it to put yourself
Last? Trust me it's harder than you think.
People This isn't a game and it's not just a
Song to be sung.

Hearts aches, hearts break and others just
Don't care but is it fair? Some people try to
Succeed but fail instead even if they're good.
Talent is not a game and it's just not a song
To be sung.

I hear the words touch upon my mind,
I hear them every day even when I am asleep.
For these words are my words; the words
Of a Poet.

It feels like this road has gone on forever,
Like I am still travelling to my destination
But I feel as if my journey has not even
Started as of yet.

Is It Only Me?

I've been in this game for so long,
Yet the best hasn't even begun,
And as I begin to ponder upon the
Thoughts which matter most
I have to know one thing.

Can you see what I see now?
Does it reflect on only me?
Oh, do you see what I see
Or is it only me?

Time and time again I go
Back and redevelop who
I am or who I could one
Day be. But my days
Are still grey while waiting
For the sunny days ahead.

Can you see what I see now?
Does it reflect on only me?
Oh, do you see what I see
Or is it only me?

It continues to flow,
It continues to run wild
And free straight out of
Me. My words could
Be your words if only
You;

Can you see what I see now?
Does it reflect on only me?
Oh, do you see what I see
Or is it only me?

This passion overdrive drives over me,
I cannot just let it be for its built in.
Yet if feels like only I can see it now
When will my chance come to wow
The pleasing crowd?

Can you see what I see now?
Does it reflect on only me?
Oh, do you see what I see
Or is it only me?

Walk by Me

Don't leave me alone in
This cruel cold dark world
I could not bear the loneliness
Which I have felt
In the years gone past.
Continue to walk by myside
In the good and bad,
Continue to walk by my side

Whether your happy or sad.
For we only have each
Other at the end of it all.
Cold comforts do
Not please the eye,
Lonesome tear drops
Pile up to the sky.
Love is not love unless
It's openly shared
Between two.
Continue to walk by myside

In the good and bad,
Continue to walk by my side
Whether your happy or sad.
For we only have each
Other at the end of it all.
Many do not last in this life,
Their split is not painless no
Matter what is said. I feel
The importance of love
And those who suffer
From a broken heart.
Continue to walk by myside

In the good and bad,
Continue to walk by my side
Whether your happy or sad.
For we only have each
Other at the end of it all.

Synthetic Moon

This world has so much fake
It could be raked up by a rake
As I wonder outside at night
I begin to see something up high.

It's real enough touch, something so tangible
Created by God himself.
For I do not see a synthetic Moon

As still as it is, it glows brightly
In my life, the patterns you
Can sometimes see could it be
Trickery of the eye?

It's real enough touch, something so tangible
Created by God himself.
For I do not see a synthetic Moon

Just to imagine the rockets blasting off
Reaching a place above us all.
The wonders of outer space
Puts me out of place in a
Place of wonder.

It's real enough touch, something so tangible
Created by God himself.
For I do not see a synthetic Moon

Better on Paper

All my efforts crumble at
The touch of my hand,
Everything I've ever set
My mind too has
Failed within my sight but
My words have stuck with me.

I'm better on paper then what I could
Ever speak, for my words are spoken
Onto paper.

You can't begin to imagine what
It's taken to get this far; I do not quit and
I do not give up in quick time.
But instead I push on because the power
Is not in spoken words.

I'm better on paper then what I could
Ever speak, for my words are spoken
Onto paper.

Every stone I could ever walk upon
Leaves a mark from my tread.
As I tread carefully upon every decision
I have had to make. As my ability keeps
on shining like a light, it has submerged me
Like water all within my mind.

I'm better on paper then what I could
Ever speak, for my words are spoken
Onto paper.

When I'm dead you'll read the best of me,
In a land that came before me and might

End after me. It's these words which might
Remain forever cherished by a nation which
Failed to acknowledge me.

I'm better on paper then what I could
Ever speak, for my words are spoken
Onto paper.

Serenade Your Heart

Let my words be filled with treasured love.
Let my words be filled with inspiring hope.
Let my words rest easy on your mind.
Let my words serenade your heart.

Let no other words come to those same effects,
Let my words hold comfort in which you seek;
Let these words of mind not be the only thing you need.
Let these words of mine serenade your heart.

For I cannot sing a sweet humble tune,
For I cannot play an instrument of any kind.
For you will not find me in an orchestra, band
Or concert hall. Let these words of
Mine serenade your heart.

For they don't blew gently in the breeze
Or bring one to their knees. They do not
Sing a song well known or often heard.
Let these words of mine serenade your heart.

Let these words be remembered for rest of time,
Let these words be told a lifetime long;
It's like my song, my story untold.
It's the truths I have lived and spoke
Openly about with an uneasy mind.
Let these words of mine serenade your heart.

To love someone openly, honesty
is the greatest gift of all, you walk a long immeasurable
distance together building up time and effort within
the relationship and you wonder why breakups are so
hard?

I adore you are beautiful, how you rise in strength,
I adore how you are determined for people to see our best.
I adore us both, this road we have walked,
for we are stronger together than ever before.
I adore this love we hold so strong
I adore your voice and its beautiful songs
like sun and moon you shine brightly in my life,
I adore the fact that you are you always.

Never Enough

If there was enough love in the
World things we be better
Then what they are but you know
As well as I do that it can
Never be. When it comes to
Loving embrace
There is never enough.

Crazy Beautiful

You're the sunshine which
Brightens my mornings,
You're the star which makes
My night twinkle bright;
Your love is my blanket in
The winter nights.
To me your crazy beautiful.

Your laughter is my happiness,
In your happiness I dwell to forget
My hell; your love is like a spell
Being cast over me.
To me your crazy beautiful.

Your command makes me move,
When you sing it puts me in the
Groove, love is never perfect
But it's perfect enough for me.
To me your crazy beautiful.

You're like my jar of mixed herbs,
Your cooking cures my starvation
When your angry your looks deepen;
You leave no word unspoken.
To me your crazy beautiful.

You bring your ideas to life,
You have brought life to my
Concepts as I gain more knowledge
Of you being you thru and thru.
To me your crazy beautiful.

I would not have you any other way
But the way I know, you are my sled
Pulling me through the snow.
Your smile has a glow.
To me your crazy beautiful.

One Glimpse of You

Life does not play a fair game,
Though it gave me a chance
Even if only for a minute, if only
For a second one glimpse of you
Would get me through

If by chance I should stumble even
More then I'd hope it would be to
Stumble over you. Even if only for a
Minute, if only for a second one
Glimpse of you would get me through

I never known beauty until I knew you,
I never knew the feeling of love until I met you
Some things never remain the same
but I know we do, even if only for a minute,
if only for a second one glimpse of you would
Get me through

Step by Step

Step by step we'll rise to the top,
Step by step I'll be holding your hand.

See where we've come
And how long it took; It serves as a reminder that
Hard work will eventually pay off.

Step by step we'll rise to the top,
Step by step I'll be holding your hand.

Positivity lights up our world, it puts a
Spark in our minds and a spring into our
Steps so that we start leaping and
Jumping About.

Step by step we'll rise to the top,
Step by step I'll be holding your hand.

Don't let go of the bigger dream
Which lies in wait,
Don't be stopped or stood
Still by hesitation, it only
Fulfils a bigger frustration into our plans.

Step by step we'll rise to the top,
Step by step I'll be holding your hand.
See where we've come

And how long it took;
It serves as a reminder that hard work
Will eventually pay off.

Step by step we'll rise to the top,
Step by step I'll be holding your hand.

A New Future

As the sun rises upon a brand-new
Day as my mind starts
To ponder upon
The possibilities
Which may lay ahead.
A new future is Brought to life.

And it's in the way we
Choose to live
It's in the decisions
That we made
Which brought a new
Future to life.

My heart always
Beats for more
It's the determination,
The forward
Thinking which brought
A new future to life.

Yet I cannot complain
At starting a
New game as we learn
To live for what
Lies ahead, for we have
Stepped out into the
Deep which brought
a new future to life.

As the sun rises upon
A brand-new
Day my mind
Starts to ponder upon the

possibilities which
May lay ahead. A new future
Is brought to life.

"I just want to glance my eyes upon
something real and beautiful like you"

Just like you, I have made mistakes in life.
I have stumbled, tripped and fallen also
but in return life has granted us all little daily
wisdom's so that we can in the future avoid
these pitfalls

The Road I'm Walking

When I think about how hard
Things are it reminds
Me of the road I'm walking down.

Sometimes are easy,
Other times being hard.
It's a mixture that goes
Into baking the cake.
Sometimes it comes out
Good while at times It comes
Out burnt or Over cooked.

When I think about how hard
Things are it reminds
Me of the road I'm walking down.

Sometimes time flies or it
Drags on into the forever,
Patients can be hard to
Process during the difficult
Times we endure.

When I think about how hard
Things are it reminds
Me of the road I'm walking down.

The strength to cope is
Often a struggle of its own,
The weakness we feel tries to
Overpower our lives
As we find ourselves
Hanging on to the dwindling
Hope.

When I think about how hard
Things are it reminds
Me of the road I'm working down.

Sometimes are easy,
Other times being hard.
It's a mixture that goes
Into baking the cake.
Sometimes it comes
Out good while at times
It comes out burnt or over cooked.

When I think about how hard
Things are it reminds
Me of the road I'm working down.

The Life We Knew

Everything I wanted to be was far from reach,
In a world I wanted to create so bad.
The lengths I went to never seemed long enough
As I gaze upon the life I thought I knew

The memories, some were good, others were not.
As my mind begins to wonder back in time remembering
Those things which have made me as
I am as I gaze Upon the life I thought I knew.

The answer to my questions are not always there,
Life is a mystery left to solve as I try not to dissolve
From the hard times I have endured as
I gaze upon A life I thought I knew.

For we continue to keep wondering into the
Unknown every day, for it's those times we
Either create something good or bad as we

All gaze upon a life we thought we knew.
Everything I wanted to be was far from reach,
In a world I wanted to create so bad.
The lengths I went to never seemed long enough
As I gaze upon the life I thought I knew

Fog

It's like fog has set upon our eyes
For we cannot see an untold future.

Life brought us together to do our best,
To create something new.

It's like fog has set upon our eyes
For we cannot see an untold future.

Losing my mind about something I can't change
Short term but hanging in their will see it's best form.

It's like fog has set upon our eyes
For we cannot see an untold future.

Every time we try it brings about the
Truths we already knew before,
Life is for the living so let's give it a lot more.

It's like fog has set upon our eyes
For we cannot see an untold future.

Fragile

Words overcome a fragile
Mind which is on the edge
Of breaking, breaking down.

As I prepare to face an uncertain
Future which does not seem stable
As I tell myself I am able

Words overcome a fragile
Mind which is on the edge
Of breaking, breaking down

The feeling rushes through
me like
Rivers ever flowing
with the might
Of the ocean waves as
I come crashing down.

Words overcome a fragile
Mind which is on the edge
Of breaking, breaking down

Understanding is not in order,
Walking that mile seems like
It's all wasted action as I start
To ponder upon the thoughts
Of weakening strength.

Words overcome a fragile
Mind which is on the edge
Of breaking, breaking down

You are everything to yourself first,
Live to better the life you live everyday

The Road We Walk

If life was always like this the challenge
Would disappear even without you near.
I'd rather walk a hard road with you
Then walk no road at all.

The things that we do are created between
Me and you, yes, it's true how I feel for you.
I'd rather walk a hard road with you
Then walk no road at all.

Everything I am, is invested into you
Everything you are is invested into me
As continue down this road we walk.
I'd rather walk a hard road with you
Then walk no road at all.

Today, I have chosen to arrive at the doorstep of my heart, to knock on
Its door because I want to know the real person living in there

Was it something in the air?
Was it something in my heart
Which began to flare?
Whatever it was maybe it just
Seemed too good to last.

When Love Begins to Die

You know it's dragged on long enough
When the love begins to die.

When you have no tears left to cry
That is when the love begins to die

And it is dying is in silent mode,
It dies within you first then outwards
It begins to show.

When the curtains do not get a chance
To open or close that's
When the love Begins to die.

When the audience does not come,
And the seats remain unfilled from
What could be the greatest show.

You know it has dragged on long enough
when the love begins to die.

A place where I can dwell in my own,
The peace it brings and its songs that it sings.
A state I much prefer, along where I
Can hide and forget the world outside

Where my thoughts are free to roam.
Some may think that I am lonely but
Keeping to myself is what I do best.
So, forget the rest.

I cannot breathe in a world of
Polluted thoughts, the negativity
Is enough to lock myself away.
Where my Solitude kicks in.

Every day I am growing,
Every day there is more
I am knowing
For I am not the man
I was yesterday.

Is it all just a state of mind? Does what we feel linger forever?
Or will it just one day fade away?

The value of a memory never passes thought
Until you sit down and begin to talk.

Made for Love

Your happiness soaked into my soul,
Your sadness dripped over me;
Your smile became my smile and it
Covered my face in an empty world.

My words fell from your lips,
Your lips which were moist as
Your tongue confessed the
Meanings of love in a natural
Flow of words but the actions
Came later.

Dwelling in your happiness was me
Trying to escape the realities which
Seemed daunting as my eyes peeked
Over the sheets beaming themselves
Into a world of love.

That love had spread into a world made
For two, tangled and mangled but shining
Through the windows of our hearts as it
Remained a distraction from the world
outside.

Her eyes remain close as she dwells
In the pondering thoughts which
Cross her mind but she does not mind
As I see a smile creep upon that
Smooth face shimmering in the light.

The light was to make everything
In the dark been seen as I pondered
about the possibilities of
Not being seen as I tried to hide
In the dark in a
World which was made for love.

Glowing Star

The cold wet drops of winter rain fall
Upon me like your love washing away
The blues we felt to be true.
As I Gaze At the stars at night I soon
Realise that you keep glowing like a star in my life.

And the hopes and burdens come together
Like in a package, for we cannot pick and
Choose what we endure every day.
As I gaze at the stars at night I soon realise that
You keep glowing like a star in my life.

Life is the story that we write day in and
Day out, for we are the Authors but
We don't know the ending, no not yet.
As I gaze at the stars at night I soon realise
That you keep glowing like a star in my life.

Call it what it is, call it life, call it love. we call it both.
For we live and love in a world known to us.

For I would not change a single thing
About you, for you're my greatest
Story, our ending is not known thank
Goodness as we continue to love
And live in a world created by us.

The cold wet drops of winter rain fall
Upon me like your love washing away
The blues we felt to be true.
As I gaze at the stars at night I soon realise
That you keep glowing like a Star in my life.

The Chances Are

As we strive to keep pushing on,
We learn that rejection is only
A mile long each time but in my
Heart the ability to keep going lives on.
The chances are the chances are gone.

There is no tear drop in the naked eye
That has not seen the hard road.
Just like me there are millions
More discovering that
The chances are the chances have gone.

How can you resist a broken heart?
When that heart has poured out
Everything it has to give.
In a world like today you
Quickly learn that the
Chances are the chances are gone.

That foot in the door just became
Another foot which is sore,
It is starting to swell up and
Bruise from endless efforts
In a cruel but dying world.
The chances are that the chances are gone.

Worlds Divided

She drifted into my world, on a ship made of love.
It gleamed through her eyes and confessed by
Her mouth.

For she sailed right in docking within my bay
But little would we know that the storms were on
Their way.

As for the storms, they ripped and tore their way in
Leaving a catastrophic mess which we almost failed
To work through.

So, we struggled to agree, our opinions did not match.
For our worlds had been divided not knowing if their
Was away to fix.

For I find it somewhat difficult just to sit back and watch
From abroad while failure torches my everlasting soul.

She drifted into my world, on a ship made of love.
It gleamed through her eyes and confessed by
Her mouth.

love and joy

Yet to Come

Thinking about how far we have come
From day one, still believing we
Made this far. For your future is yet
To come even more

And he shows more potential every day,
He is growing and learning in a whole new
Way and in ways which are unknown to
Us. For his future is yet to come even more.

I might write the words of meaning, the
Words which express but it is never the
Easiest way. For my future is yet to come
Even more.

We cannot see the road ahead, we do not always
Know everything and yes, we are learning more
And more as we live our best out every day.
For our future as a family is yet to come
Even more.

Thinking about how far we have come
From day one, still believing we
Made this far. For your future is yet
To come even more

Until You Came Along

My skies were not blue
Until I met you,
Loneliness sung
Right through
No purpose shone upon
Until you came along
And wrote my song.

My days were not counted,
My life was discarded.
My mind was rubbished
With sad thoughts until
You came along and
Wrote my song.

And now that you
Are near
It has put to end to all
The above as I dwell
In your love since
You came along
And wrote my song.

Waiting for My Time

I am sitting on the sidelines waiting for my shot,
I am patiently waiting for my time to come.
I am standing around feeling wasted, when will I sprout?
I am patiently waiting for my time to come.

It is the agonising period of life
I am patiently waiting for my time to come.
Spinning, rotating and angling my views of life
I am patiently waiting for my time to come.

Standing on the shores watching
The waters once more
I am patiently waiting for my time to come.

My words sit on my mind
Waiting to be spoken while
I am patiently waiting for my time to come.

The love is felt only within,
For it is not shared while
I am patiently waiting for my time to come.

My mind is like a garden bed,
My words sprout like wildflowers.
I am Patiently waiting for my time to come.

A Touch of Heaven

My days of trying seems to grow old
They have become the efforts of this cold
Dark World. I am waiting for the touch of
Heaven to press against my life.

For my thoughts are my greatest enemy
I have encountered yet, the defeatist
Attitudes which linger in a
life hard lived. I am waiting for a touch of
Heaven to press against my life.

And the roads we walk would be better
Less travelled but if they were
Then who would we be?
I am waiting for the touch of
Heaven to press against my life.

Yet the yoke in my heart continues
To spill out onto paper as I live
For better days but those better
Days need to come while I am
Waiting for a touch of Heaven
To press against my life.

I thought I would know
A life different to this,
But the path I am walking
Has not yet changed and
I cannot change it without
Waiting for a touch of Heaven
To press against my l

State of Mind

Something as real as this cannot be played with;
Something so fragile, it is not hit and miss.
For it affects us all in so many ways, it will make
You laugh, shout, scream or cry.

It carries the thoughts which result in action,
This is why we need to be clear minded.
For it affects us all in so many ways, it will make
You laugh, shout, scream or cry.

Yet do not be quick to judge or tease,
But be the first to bring ease.
What have you got to gain when
It's someone else you slain?
For it affects us all in so
Many ways, it will make
You laugh, shout, scream or cry.

We need to lift others up,
Be the first to give the chance
To help them rise too their
Feet and start to dance.
For it affects us all in so
Many ways, it will make
You laugh, shout, scream or cry.

Never forget where you have come from
Or how long it took you to come this far,
In a world where they murder your spirit
And judge your character. Failure is real,
Real enough to touch.

For it affects us all in so
Many ways, it will make
You laugh, shout, scream or cry.

The Greatest Minds

This world wouldn't know something good
If they tripped over it, for we spend our
Live's, our whole Live's working on a
Dream. For it's the greatest minds
Which are rejected.

Like a parking metre we'll eventually
Expire and run out of time, this is why
We live our future right now, For it's the
Greatest minds which are rejected.

And do you think time is an issue when
Your dead when you die it's no longer
A matter of ours. It's only our matter
While we're still living. For it's the
Greatest minds which are rejected.

Rise up! And take up the positivity
To keep trying, this world will lay
Judgement therefore there is no
Need to judge yourself. We are
Defined by what we do and not
Who we are.

Your importance may not be
Recognized, seen, heard or felt.
But that does not mean it's not
In existence, for the existence
Of you is enough to bring about
Your course of survival. For it's the
Greatest minds which are rejected.

Dreams Turn to Nightmares

They say that you sleep in the bed you've made
But it's more than just that, for I am tossing
Around remaining unsettled in a dreaming
Destiny.

Turning; screaming, yelling being haunted just
Watching my dreams turn to nightmares.

When I thought it was possible to wake
When I thought it was possible to rest easy;
When I thought the worst had past it's
Then I started

Turning; screaming, yelling being haunted just
Watching my dreams turn to nightmares.

Not even a morning coffee could cure this start,
As I prepared for what could lay ahead. The
Truths which I have seen unfold and the belief I must carry
To get ahead.

Turning; screaming, yelling being haunted just
Watching my dreams turn to nightmares.

And as I made my bed each morning, the wrinkles
Were seen in its sheets, although it seemed simple
It never looked perfect.

Turning; screaming, yelling being haunted just
Watching my dreams turn to nightmares.

Without a dream there is no purpose
But it gets to the point where you enter

Shock horror just realizing each and
Every day what lies in wait.

Turning; screaming, yelling being haunted just
Watching my dreams turn to nightmares.

They say that you sleep in the bed you've made
But it's more than just that, for I am tossing
Around remaining unsettled in a dreaming
Destiny.

Turning; screaming, yelling being haunted just
Watching my dreams turn to nightmares.

Roses

My roses are not red, neither are they blue
But they have turned the colour of grey
From a world which failed to love them
While their hopes of being picked
Diminished and died.

If your roses are not picked, don't discourage
Just get up and plant a new bunch.

My garden bed is damp, it's been watered
Long enough; the sunshine has beamed down
It's starting to dry out. The colours in my petals
Brighten up my life.

If your roses are not picked, don't discourage
Just get up and plant a new bunch.

For you won't see them in a shop for the world
To see, instead just standing around, sitting
Around waiting to be picked.

If your roses are not picked, don't discourage
Just sit and patiently wait.

My roses are not red, neither are they blue
But they have gone the colour of grey
From a world which failed to love them
While their hopes of being picked
Diminished and died.

For My Love Will Not

As the thoughts of an approaching
Summer crosses my mind
Winter left a chill down my spine and
Autumn did not make
Me fall.

As the seasons come and go,
As the seasons change;
For my love will not.

As the rains pelts down,
As the lightening cracks
And the thunder roars.
Just remember

As the seasons come and go,
As the seasons change;
For my love will not.

As the spring brings it ways
It could put me in a warm daze;
But it does not and cannot last
Any longer than the love which
We hold.

As the seasons come and go,
As the seasons change;
For my love will not.

To Break My Heart

How do I find the strength in the world as such as ours?
The battles we have fought and the battles we still need
To fight. I've loved and lived in a world which continues
Even more to break my heart.

For I can't trust this world of greedy, unlawful ways which
Conflict against us in all we do. I have tried and
Tried to forget the heartaches in a world which continues
Even more to break my heart.

Lifting your head high while walking in the shame
They try to put on you, rejection bleeds out
Heavily. It doesn't matter anymore if your
Good at what you do in a world which continues
Even more to break my heart.

Our subsistence does not and has not mattered
In a time before now, they're not quick to deal
Out good opportunities so what difference
Does it really make in a world which continues
Even more to break my heart.

Yet in your eyes I am deemed a fool for trying,
How it seemed like time wasted for me.
For I just can't let go of a dream that quickly
In a world which continues even more
To break my heart.

Stand in my shoes just for a moment
How would you feel? How could it be
Possible to end up this way?

You can spend time and money
But just end up lying
There bleeding out in a world which continues
Even more to break my heart.

In A Lonely Forbidden World

My next line came from deep thought, the thoughts
Which did not matter in a passing world; my world.
It was passing me quicker then what I could
Have expected in a lonely forbidden world.

Did you not see me? Was my voice not loud
Enough when I shouted and screamed?
You speak of let downs, but It was passing
Me quicker than what I could have expected
In a lonely forbidden world.

You think your all that?
Let's think twice about that.
For you shut the door so
dam tight that not even you
Could get back in if you
Had ever ended back outside.
It all seemed to real
In a lonely forbidden world.

My tear drops are not formed in love but
In vile hate and anger from a time where
My purposes had diminished, fallen, tossed
Out as It was passing me quicker then
What I could have expected in a
Lonely forbidden world.

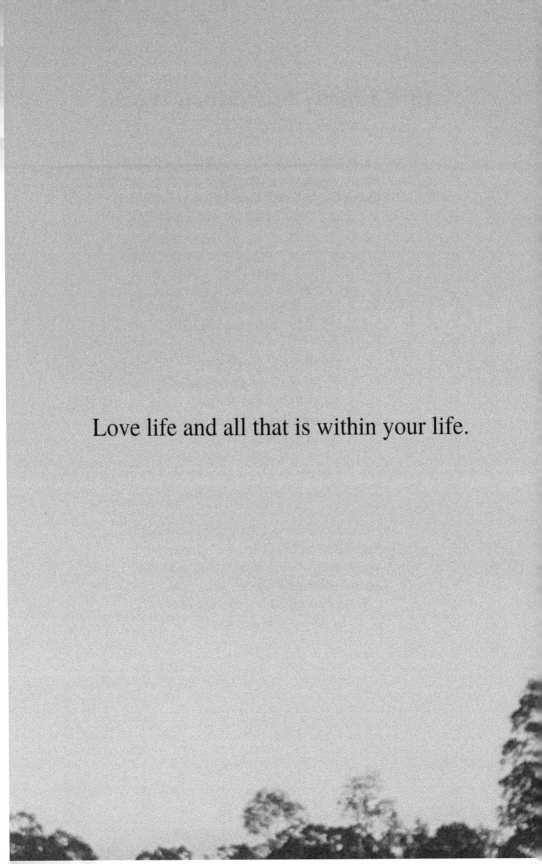

Love life and all that is within your life.

Dreams and Realities

In the dreaming depths of reality did
we somehow cross over
To the point where we could not
be brought back?

In the dreams we wanted,
in the realities which are.

It's where two world mix into one.
Like a fantasy gone wrong,
where the mind sings its own song,
To the point where we could not
be brought back.

In the dreams we wanted,
In the realities which are

It's where two world mix into one.
A place of drifting thought or did I drift
before the thought became a thought
In what I thought to be good to the point
where we could not be brought back

In the dreams we wanted,
In the realities which are

It's where two world mix into one.
Totally consumed, submerged, and defined
In a world I thought could be mine
Yet in that world I could not dine.

In the dreams we wanted,
In the realities which are

It's where two world mix into one.
In the dreaming depths of reality did
we somehow cross over
To the point where we could not
be brought back?

The Difference

Somethings we made to never be
The same ever again as we live to
Find the difference in me and you.

She took my hand somewhat years ago,
Like me she had nothing but a dream in
Her heart as we both wanted to live to
Find the difference in us both.

For it's the roads which we must walk,
Sometimes not easy but can at times be fun-
Yet the challenges lie in wait they do not
Hesitate that's when we find
The difference in us all.

Our personalities reflect upon
Others greatly, sometimes
We don't realize that at first.
For when we face others
For they too can see the
Difference in me and you.

I don't live to be the same, nor do I live
My life in repeat. For I constantly strive
To keep refreshing my life, and what I do.
And I hope that you can see the difference
In me as you read these words.

In a Life We Built Together

You drifted into my life,
As if you were floating
In the breeze-
you brought the gift of love
In a life we built together.

I was a broken man
And you were a broken girl
For we fixed each other's
Worlds in a life we built
Together.

For it was not easy to do
But look how far we've come
In a time where impossibilities
Become possible in a life we
Built together.

So just remember when the seas
Are rough or our nights are cold
That we as one came this far by
Believing that the impossible could
Be possible in a life we built together.

Accepting the Unacceptable

All my life I have given my loyalty to all the wrong people and
now I have ended up at the bottom.
Yet I have loved with an unconditional love, I have worked
and given my all. But you learn that the problem is not
being loyal it is them not being loyal to you. You cannot make
someone love you,
show kindness or fairness, it has to be given by them wanting
to give it. If they choose not to then that is it.
You can scream, yell, get mad or even beg but it will not
change the condition of their heart.
They have aligned their heart with their mind, the pain you feel
is that hurt, regret just thinking that if you had done
something differently, it may have lasted. You are left feeling
as if you did something
wrong when you know you did not. It is not fair, but its life and
life just isn't fair to some people.
Just keep being strong, you are under strength and ability to
move on will are the rising of new skyscraper
that will be indestructible.

I sit there watching her eat a bowl of salad,
She content, happy and peaceful because she's in
Love and she has her own little joys which
Make her night what it is. Do what makes you
happy, what brings you simple little joys.

Every day I make a new decision within myself to look forward, to
start again reminding myself that those who couldn't see my light
shine
were wrong and that this day I have made mine so I
can once more look outwards into those new horizons,
take a deep breath and smile

Without arms to hold you, you are always

Strong, beautiful, and resilient

Be fruitful in your ambitions, dreams are not born overnight but over years of hard work and long-suffering.
If you're only in something for money then you won't last the distance. Be willing to enter the deep waters because how can you allow your whole body to be completely submerged in what you do if you only get your ankles wet? Failing is the true road to success

You are amazing because despite everything life throws in you're path you have manage to overcome it, it may not happen straight away, but its effects will be seen bit by bit. Every lesson you have learnt from cannot be taught in schools or educational institutions, it can only be learnt by living life. Give yourself more credit because you my friend are self-taught

Understand myself was learning that all the negative opinions from others were all just whispers in the wind eventually they'll blow away

Do you remember those taunting dreams
which echo throughout your mind?
How they seemed so real and how
you woke up almost dropping to the floor.
Life is full of experiences we
love and dislike but nevertheless we still
have to endure them until they end.

I want to keep feeling something real like life,
To see the end of pain and the start of new beginnings.
To see this story never end as well as having someone
Like yourself as a friend.

Strong People

Have

Difficult Lives

But Still

Survive

love to sit outside in the warmth of the sun and listen to the birds, coffee piping hot; maybe a slight breeze. I love to daze at the white scattered clouds and form pictures with them in my imagination. There are days I love the pitta patter of the rain, falling against the roof of a house, just watching a great magnitude of water falling upon us just soaking In its downpour just like I soak in the downpour of her love which rains upon me every day as I long to just keep getting lost in her world, in the warmth of her sun listening to her songs as if she were a bird perched upon my branch.

Understand her mind, be sensitive to her needs.
Show her your gently touch maybe then you'll
gain her heart

Watch her glow at night
And sparkle in the sunlight

Her touch,

Her style

Her humour,

Her laugh.

Her love is

Built to last

Sensual feelings, fluttering whispers pulling me in with her suction of love as I lose my grip hanging from her cliff dangling off her edge I'm about to drop and free fall into her arms.

Remember who's in your heart
And how hard it was to place them there

You hold me in a world which left scars, you nurture me when
Love seems too hard as you clothe in the kindness,
Sweetest love which I believe dreams are made of.

It was always you from the start, everything about you
Was everything a man like me needed

I never thought I could be loved
Until you came along and showed me
That dreams really do come true

We both were searching for the same thing
Unknowingly knowing we would find it in
Each other, love found us.

The good part is that I don't know
How to let you go

My heart will not grow old with a
Refreshing love you give

blossoming into a
Beautiful rose that someone
One day will pick

Moment's bring us together as family, as friends. They also create the finest and bad parts of life, every moment is priceless like the times we spend together watching movies on rainy days, afternoon walks along the beach and the times, I spend loving you.

Here's the thing, she could've loved anybody
But she chose me

If you're looking for an easy love,
I'm sorry, it doesn't exist

I soak in your desire,
A passionate fire-
Lips trembling across each other
Weakened by your beauty
A tale of romance unfolds
In ways untold

My longing was longing to hold someone
Just like you in my arms

I've always craved the words in my mind,
Dug deep to find their life.
Held them close just to feel their love and strength
But I had to let them go just for you
To cherish as you can see they were never
Really mine

You fall deep into the desire in your mind,
The romantic thoughts which keep you alive
Believing that there is still hope and time
For you to love someone just as much as
You love yourself

Opportunities don't often come, so embrace them with open arms and with an open heart. This way you will love it more while making the most of something you enjoy.

The good things in life are more likely to hurt us then the things
We don't love us much

When you laugh at my idiocy that makes me
Feel special, the kind of special which only
Comes from you

Love is a gift, make sure if you give it;
It won't be returned or exchanged

Be in someone else's every
Second

There is something beautiful about life itself;
The way you love me and all my imperfections

It was the first time we held hands, gazed into each other's eyes
While leaning in for that first kiss which brought about years of
Happiness but you still don't forget that first moment, that lasts a
Lifetime

I was one of those guys who
Who couldn't bear to be alone
So, I searched and found a good
Girl of my own

Love can take years to discover, but when you
Find that special love you will have found a love
Which glows within just for you

Do not ever stand for abuse, abuse does not
Show love, it destroys it

I'm happy today because…

Becoming you is never easy, it's a work in progress.
Every single day you progress forward to becoming a
Better you.

You may have days you find hard to face,
But that's ok. Be strong everything will get
Better.

When you've lived in a world of loneliness for so
Long, it's hard to imagine love but trust me it really
Does exist.

If someone exits your entry through point
Don't worry, one day you'll find a keeper, an actual keeper of your
Heart

Be bold, take chances you have nothing to lose by having ago, try to remain optimistic when you face challenges. It's only by trying and accepting our failures can we eventually succeed. Remember, it's all in you. It always has been.

Try not to see mistakes or bad choices totally in a negative
Light, but use it as a learning curve, a guidance tool to
Better yourself for the future. Without making mistakes how
Would we learn? Remember this next time you feel failure.

Strength comes from being
Broken

Love isn't something you just pass out to anyone, it's something sacred, special, and lasting. It's an incredibly special friendship between two people who are inseparable, who want to grow old together and still be able to share that magical kiss
Many years later.

Life is all about discovering you as a person,
What you love, dislike, what to hold dear and what
To let go but never let go of you for you hold much more
Value over another object in your life

I often wonder what life could have been, but then I remember this;
If it wasn't for the road I have walked, the struggles I have endured
I wouldn't be the person I am today.

Sometimes the hardest thing to do
Is to know what comes next.

You cry in dark places because
That's where sorrow meets you.

I know you hurt at times and I know you struggle.
You may find it hard to love, being at work or in general everyday
life. But I am here to tell You it only gets better; you jus
t need a little faith, belief, and hope.

Love

It's something we all need

You have loved me like no
One ever could

I have never known a love like the
Love I have found in you

My heart is the drum that plays
The beat to her song

Did you know that when I close my eyes I see you in my dreams,
that dream then
Transforms into a reality when I awake

She loves all the simple things like me,
The picnics at the beach and laughing
At my silliness. I love it!

All her little dramas draw me closer to her in
More beautiful ways than you'll ever know.

Love is like a flower
You plant the seed, water it and watch it
Grow into something special.

.

A love expressed is a love felt,
A love unexpressed is a love which
Dies.

I had to learn to live life on my own
But I learnt how to love life after meeting
You.

Let the tears fall, let the heart break because after all that You'll be a stronger, wiser and more beautiful person worth Loving.

She whispered the secrets which drew me closer and
Closer revealing what I had believed all along.
She loved me.

Do you remember the first time you fell in love?
It was liked you had stepped into a brand-new world.
A whole new bunch of feelings, indescribable joys,
It's like the first time as a child at an amusement park
You just don't want to leave.

The soft silky feel of a rose petal
Rubbing between my fingers brings a
Sense of love as I close my eyes and let
My imagination run wild.

Always Trust in God

He is greater than all of us.

If you are searching for love then remember this,
You need to know you first. Find out what you really
Want, this way you will know what to seek.

I am grateful today because…

I have woken up and been giving another
Day to express my love to you.

Remember to cherish every moment in life
Because one day we wake up and those moments and
People in our lives have either grown up or passed away
And our chances have past as well.

You are always loved by someone even if you
Can't feel it

Let the heart break, let the pain hurt.
This is how we grow

Failure only means that we haven't discovered
Our right pathway which leads to success

Appreciate the beauty of the sunrise and sunsets,
Appreciate the smell of beautiful flowers in spring.
Appreciate the massive blue ocean and its waves,
Appreciate life while you can

Beautiful,

That's how I've always seen
You

She flipped through the pages only to
Discover her life in the book she was
Reading

All she wanted was for you to step out,
Walk across her surface as if it were
The first moon landing.

You are too beautiful to hurt,
So, life your head and wipe your eyes
For tomorrow is yet another day to set
Sail your heart to foreign shores which awaits
A beautiful ship like yours.

Let your love speak words of whispers
Which transform into love poetry.

Learn to accept yourself, learn to be happy with who
You have become and
know that while self-improvement
Is always possible it still takes time,
give yourself time, don't
Be in a rush or the results you are
 hoping for will be unpleasing

I want the embers of my dying fire
To flare up and keep you warm in a
Cold world.

I caught her smiling when she thought
I wasn't watching.

You are the most beautiful aspect
About yourself.

Why does love have to be so complicated
When it was designed to be simple.

Home is always in Your heart.

Never forget the great distance you have walked
To become you.

True love holds a value
Which can't be valued

She looked up at the night sky and believed
She was up there glowing with the stars
Even though she was covered in darkness.

Love was more than what I expected,
It brought me a lifetime of you.

She walked in pride because she knew
Wherever she went, she was loved.

The deeper we fell into love,
There was no way out.

I crave your touch, thirst for your desire.
Sense your touch, fall deeper for your love.
Quench my thirst, feed my starvation, fill
My emptiness with all you are.

You just can't expect love, but you have to give it, show it, practise it every single day and then it'll come in ways you will not expect. Love is more than having someone constantly beside you but it's all the little things you do for family, friends and other little special people in your life.

We all long for things we can't have,
As flowers we blossom but somehow
Our hearts weep, wilt and die.

I just need you,
Don't ask why
Just know that I do!

Just as the sun and moon belong to the sky,
You belong to me.